Stories from the World War II Battlefield

World War II Writing Prompts

Jennifer Holik

Also By Jennifer Holik

Faces of War: Researching Your Adopted Soldier

*Stories from the World War II Battlefield Volume 3:
Writing the Stories of War*

*Stories from the World War II Battlefield Volume 2:
Navigating Service Records for the
Navy, Coast Guard, Marine Corps, and Merchant Marine*

*Stories from the World War II Battlefield Volume 1:
Reconstructing Army, Air Corps, and
National Guard Service*

*Stories from the Battlefield: A Beginning Guide to
World War II Research*

The Tiger's Widow

Stories of the Lost

*Engaging the Next Generation:
A Guide for Genealogy Societies and Libraries*

Branching Out: Genealogy for Adults

Branching Out: Genealogy for High School Students

Branching Out: Genealogy for 4th-8th Grades Students

Branching Out: Genealogy for 1st-3rd Grade Students

To Soar with the Tigers

Copyright Information

Copyright © 2016 Jennifer Holik
Publisher: Generations, Woodridge, Illinois

All rights reserved. No part of this book may be reproduced or transmitted in any form or by any means, electronic or mechanical, including photocopying, recording, or by any information storage or retrieval system without written permission from the author, except for the inclusion of brief quotations in a review.

Editor: Logan Ausmus.
Cover Designer: Sarah Sucansky.

Holik, Jennifer, 1973 –
    Stories from the World War II Battlefield: World War II Writing Prompts / Jennifer Holik. Includes bibliographical references and indexes.

ISBN: 1-938226-38-0
ISBN-13:978-1-938226-38-0

Printed in the United States of America

Dedication

To all who research, write, and share stories about World War II. Through all our efforts, the stories of the those who lived during the war years will not be forgotten.

Acknowledgments

All my love and thanks to my three wonderful boys for listening to me talk about this project for the last year. I appreciate your patience and feedback on what I was trying to do.

Thank you to Johan van Waart for his encouragement, support, feedback, and love as I finished this project.

A huge thank you to my amazing cover designer, Sarah Sucansky. She has again created a beautiful cover for my book. My editor Logan Ausmus for editing this volume.

Thank you Andrew Speese for giving me permission to use your photo on the cover. Thank you to Eric Bijtelaar and Jim Hooper for providing feedback on the writing prompts.

Table of Contents

Acknowledgments	ix
Purpose	1
Writing Prompts - United States	5
Writing Prompts - Europe	21
Writing Prompts - Veterans	37
Writing Prompts - Children and Grandchildren of War	45
Writing Prompts - Visiting The Theaters of War	53
Additional Resources	59
About The Author	65

Purpose

Purpose

Stories help us preserve the past and provide hope that history will not repeat itself. For some cultures, storytelling is the primary method for transmitting a family or group's collective history. For others, writing the stories to share with family or the world, is the method.

Writing is an activity we were taught at a young age. Our parents and teachers showed us how to write our alphabet and string those letters together to form words. Those words formed sentences and sentences formed paragraphs. Once we knew how to do this, writing took many forms. We used those forms to write for school, work, in personal diaries and journals, letters, emails, and for use on social media.

At the end of the day, we must ask ourselves, what writing really matters? What writing will be our legacy? What writing can we share to document our lives, those who have gone before us, and those who survived a time when the world was collapsing in chaos?

People often think they need the whole story, all their questions answered, or all the research completed before they can begin writing. This is not true. We can begin writing with very little and add to the story as we locate new information. As we write, gaps in information and errors appear throughout the process. This is normal and helpful because research and writing are a process. Part of the process is rewriting again and again, until the story that wants to be told …. Is.

I feel it is important to listen, capture, research, and write the stories of our World War II fallen, veterans, and civilians, before they are gone. Do not leave this work to the next generation, for they may ignore the call.

The purpose of this book is to provide writing prompts for World War II to help you think about your family's stories. If you need more structured assistance in writing the stories of war, please pick up a copy of

Purpose of Book

my *Stories from the World War II Battlefield Volume 3: Writing the Stories of War* book. It includes:

- Reasons to write the stories of war.
- Tips to help you organize your thoughts and sources before you write.
- Writing formulas to help you organize your stories.
- More than 500 writing prompts covering multiple themes for writers in the U.S. and overseas.
- Suggestions on how to share your stories on memorial websites and through books.
- Additional resources for writing the stories of war.

I hope this writing prompt book inspires you to start writing your World War II stories.

Writing Prompts - United States

Life on the Home Front Before the War

1. Describe life before the war. Consider education, jobs, and the roles of men, women and children in your family.
	a. What jobs did your father hold?
	b. Did your mother work outside the house?
	c. Did anyone in your extended family live with/near you?
	d. Did the children in the family help with chores in the house or work outside the house to help support the family?

2. How did your family survive the Great Depression? How did things change for them as the war approached?

3. Did your family have a tradition of military service? If so, who served and in what wars or conflicts?

4. What kind of entertainment did the family enjoy prior to the war? Did they own a radio? Go to the theater or museums?

5. Describe the clothing, hair, and shoe styles prior to the war.
	a. Do you have photographs to illustrate how your family dressed?
	b. Did your family wear the latest fashions?

6. Describe the technology available prior to the war.
	a. How did this change during the war? What new technology became available?
	b. How did this change after the war? What new technology became available?

Life on the Home Front During the War

1. Describe life during the war for your family. In what ways did things change?
    a. What jobs did your father hold?
    b. Did your mother work outside the house?
    c. Did anyone in your extended family live with/near you?
    d. Did the children in the family help with chores in the house or work outside the house to help support the family?

2. Did anyone from your immediate family serve in the war? Who? What branch? What job did they have in the military? Did they survive the war?

3. Did anyone in your extended family serve in the war? Who? What branch? What job did they have in the military? Did they survive the war?

4. What impact did losing these family members to military service have on your family?

5. Did any men in your family NOT serve in the military and go to war? Why?

6. How did the community treat the men in your family who did not go fight?

7. What was the sendoff like for your soldier by the family or community?

8. Did any women in your family join the military? How did your family react to this?
    a. If women did serve, then in which branch?
    b. What was their job?

Writing Prompts - United States

9. Did any women in your family work in factories or take other jobs vacated by men? What jobs did they take? How did your family react to this change?

10. Describe how your family dealt with rationing during the war.
    a. What did they learn to live without?
    b. What recipes did they create to adjust to shortages in items like sugar?
    c. How did they change their lifestyles to adjust to changes?

11. Did your family have a car prior to the war? If so, was it driven much during the war or did the gasoline and rubber (tire) rationing affect the use of the car?

12. Did your family own a business during the war? What kind of business?
    a. How did rationing affect the business?
    b. How did the war affect the business? Were there miltary contracts or benefits to the owners for having this business?

13. Did you have family living in Europe or the Pacific during the war?
    a. Did they try to emigrate prior to the war?
    b. How did that affect the family?
    c. What was communication with them like during the war?
    d. How did the war change your families?

14. Did any of your female relatives lose a husband during the war? How did she deal with this loss? Did they have children? How did she support her children after his death?

15. How did the women in your family handle their boyfriends or husbands return from war? Were they changed mentally, emotionally, or physically? How did everyone handle this?

16. During the war, how did clothing, shoes, and hairstyles change? Do you have photographs to add to your story to illustrate these changes?

17. Were any children in your family born during or after the war? How was their youth different from siblings born before the war?

Writing Prompts - United States

18. Music often takes people back to specific times and places. Many new songs were released during the war to raise morale. Are there any songs that were special to your family? What were they and why were they special or important?

Community Impact

1. Describe the impact the community where your family lived had on the war effort. How many men and women did they send off to fight and serve?

2. Were there enforced blackout hours each night? How did your family and community adjust to this change?

3. Did any of your family member serve in jobs, volunteer or paid, to watch for enemy planes or submarines?

4. How did the education change in schools for children?
    a. Did they learn what to do in case of an air attack?
    b. Did they learn how to spot enemy planes?
    c. Did they learn how to recycle materials and hold recycling drives?

5. Did the community hold war bond rallies? Who participated in these events?
    a. Was there coverage in the newspaper you can use to build your family's story?

6. How did rationing affect the community?

7. Did the community have a war plant? What kind of manufacturing did this plant do?
    a. Did any of your relatives work in a war plant or support the war effort through their job?
    b. Was the work done at this war plant top secret?
    c. Was the plant built specifically for the war or taken over from another manufacturer (for example, the factory made cars and then made planes.)

8. How did the community come together to support their troops and each other during the war?

9. In what ways did women change the community when men left to fight?

10. How did the community change when the war was over and the men returned?

Women in the War

1. Did any of your female soldiers join the military or Red Cross during WWII?
    a. Which branch?
    b. What job did she hold?
    c. Where did she train?
    d. Did she serve overseas? Where and when?

2. Examine the reasons why a woman joined the Armed Forces in WWII. What did she contribute?

3. How did the family react to the woman joining the military or Red Cross? Were any women disowned?

4. After the war ended, did she remain in service? If not, what course did her life take and how did it change?
    a. Did she return home to marry or resume her married life?
    b. Did she get a job outside the house and remain single?

5. A lot is written about men in World War II but have you considered women were just as powerful as men during WWII? Write a brief piece on how you viewed your female soldiers as powerful during WWII.

Writing Prompts - United States

Military Service

1. Was your soldier drafted or did he or she enlist in the military?

2. Where did he or she train?

3. Discuss basic training and other specialized training through which your soldier went after being inducted in the service.

4. Did your soldier get a furlough while he was in the states? How long did it last? Where did he or she go? What did he or she do?

5. Write about the gear your soldier typically carried.

6. Do you have any letters, diaries, photographs, or post cards from your military soldier? Write about their service using these items.

7. Did your relative serve in the U.S. only?
    a. In what branch?
    b. Where and what was his job?
    c. How did his or her job aid the war effort?
    d. Was there any reaction from the family or community for this individual NOT going overseas to serve?

8. Was your soldier shipped overseas?
    a. To which theater(s) of war?
    b. When did they leave and when did they return?

9. Describe the living conditions of your relatives during their military service. Did he or she sleep in a tent; barracks; bombed out buildings; on the frozen ground? How often did they get a hot meal or a shower?

10. Each battleground was different. The D-Day beaches were different terrain than the Ardennes Forest or North Africa or Korea or the air over Germany. Describe the locations where he or she moved from place to place during the war.

11. Were any of your relatives taken as a Prisoner of War? What was their experience? Did they survive the war?

Writing Prompts - United States

12. Describe the down time during the war. When the front line had moved or there was no battle to fight. What did your soldier do to pass the time?

13. Discuss the transportation of troops and supplies during their service. If you have more than one soldier who fought in the same war or a different war, compare and contrast the transportation available.

14. Did your soldier have any illnesses, accidents, or wounds during the war?

15. Did your soldier serve in multiple theaters of war?
    a. With which Division(s)
    b. What was that experience like?

16. When the war ended in Europe, did your soldier have to return to the U.S. for training before being shipped to the Pacific Theater of War?
    a. Describe this process of going from Europe to the U.S. to the Pacific.
    b. How did the combat differ between theaters of war?

17. Did your soldier die in service? Have you obtained the records to tell that story?
    a. Were any personal effects returned to the family? Which ones? Do you still have them?
    b. What is the story behind the effects?

Race and Ethnicity

1. Consider how ethnicity and race affected people during WWII. For example, during World War II in the United States, Japanese Americans were sent to internment camps and African-Americans were segregated in the armed forces. Did this affect your family? How?

2. Did any member of your family have alien immigration status when the war started? How did that affect when they served in the military, if they did, and how did it affect their future naturalization?

Writing Prompts - United States

3. During the war, immigration was denied to Italians, Japanese, Germans, and Jews. Did your family experience this? How did they handle it? Were they able to immigrate after the war?

4. Is your family Jewish? What was their WWII experience? Did they share their stories?
    a. How did their experience shape your life?
    b. If they left Europe before the war, what happened to their families?
    c. What did they endure in the U.S. while the war was fought in Europe?
    d. If they remained in Europe - what was their story?

Religion and the War

1. Did your family's religion affect whether or not they served in the war? How?

2. Did anyone in your family not serve because of their religious beliefs? What were those beliefs and how did this individual avoid serving?

3. Did anyone in the family serve as a conscientious objector in the war and not carry a gun? Think about those who were medics like Desmond Doss who refused to carry a gun but still served.

4. If anyone in your family chose not to serve, how did the rest of the family deal with this decision? What conflicts did this decision cause, if any?

Communication

1. During World War I and II, word traveled to civilians primarily by mail and telegram. On the battlefield, communication was primarily by messenger and telephone. It took weeks before families were notified of wounds, Prisoner of War, Missing in Action or Killed in Action statuses. Today the communication is almost instantaneous because of cell phones and the internet. Write about communication during the war as it relates to your family.

2. Newspapers can add a lot of details to a soldier's story beyond that of his service. Think about the battles fought, the terrain, the enemy, and the weather. Use newspapers for facts that add depth to a story.
> a. Did your soldier fight on D-Day or in the Battle of the Bulge? Perhaps in the Pacific?
> b. Locate stories about the weather for major battles in which your soldier fought. Write a scene using the weather to tell a battle story.

3. Do you have any letters, VMail, diaries, photographs, or post cards from your military soldier? Write about their service using these items.

Propaganda

1. What kind of propaganda did you see or hear about the war? Photos, articles, radio broadcasts?

2. How did that help or hinder support for the war or anger toward the enemy?

3. Did anyone in your family help create propaganda during the war? Speak at a war bond drive or on the radio? Write an article for the newspaper or a magazine?

Holidays and Celebrations

1. How did your family celebrate holidays, birthdays, and anniversaries during the war years?
> a. What were the meals like as compared to before the war?
> b. What were gifts like as compared to before the war?

2. How did your soldier celebrate the holidays while he was at war? Did he have a hot meal on a major holiday?

3. Do you have any letters or photographs from soldiers that talk about the holidays? Use these to add to your soldier's story.

Writing Prompts - United States

V-E and V-J Day

1. Where were your family members on VE Day and VJ Day? Where was your soldier?

2. Did you celebrate the end of the war in Europe? The end in Pacific when ended the total war? How?

After The War

1. What the homecoming like for your soldier? Was there a community parade? A celebration at home or something quiet?

2. What did your soldier come home to when his or her service ended? Marriage? A job? Family? College? Did he or she enlist to serve again?

3. After soldiers returned, did they talk about their experiences in war? Did anyone listen? Did they share the stories with their children and grandchildren?

4. How or did your family resume a normal life?

5. Did any of your family members move from the city to the country or vice versa?

6. Did any of your family members immigrate to another country after the war?

7. How did the soldiers cope with the trauma of war?

8. How did the families cope with the trauma of war?

9. Did your family members who were Killed In Action return after the war or did they remain buried overseas?
    a. What happened to the personal effects?
    b. Were there obstacles encountered in trying to obtain effects or have the remains returned or buried overseas?
    c. Were there any family struggles if the widow remarried and the next-of-kin status reverted back to the soldier's parent?

Writing Prompts - United States

10. Did someone in your family lose a spouse and remarry?
    a. Were there blended families?
    b. Was the father who was Killed In Action remembered or was his memory tucked away in a shoebox in a closet?

11. How did the roles of women in your family change after the war ended? Or did life resume as it was with women returning to the old roles?

12. After the war, men were still required to register with Selective Service and serve in the military a compulsory two years. The compulsory two year service ended in the late 1960s. Did the patriotism and desire to join the military become instilled in every generation that followed? Or did the men not wish to serve and fight? Explain.

13. How did the WWII era affect your family from then until now?

War Orphans and Adoption

1. If your father killed in the war, did your mother remarry? How did you feel about that?

2. Did your step-father adopt you? How did you feel about that?

3. If your mother did not remarry, how did she support you and, if applicable, your siblings? Did she move back in with her family?

4. Was your father discussed as you grew up or was it a topic that was not discussed?

5. When did you learn about your father's service? What information, stories, or photographs helped you piece together his story?

6. Did you ever use his GI Bill to attend college? How did that change your life?

Remembrance of the Fallen

1. If your soldier is buried overseas, did anyone adopt his or her grave? If so, are you in contact with the individual or family?

2. If your soldier is buried overseas, how is his or her memory honored by the cemetery?

3. Do you honor those in your family who died in military service on Memorial Day? How?

4. Do you have any stories or photographs of Memorial Days from years past? Particularly immediately after the war when families would visit cemeteries more often?

5. Does your community honor the fallen? How?

6. Did you ever visit your fallen soldier who remained buried overseas or is listed on a Wall of the Missing? If so, what prompted you to take that trip overseas?

Honoring the Veterans

1. Do you honor those in your family who survived the war on Veterans Day? How?

2. Does your community honor its veterans? How?

Memories of Post-War Generations

1. What memories do you have of your parents, grandparents, or other family members telling you about the war? What stories did they tell you?

2. Do you have any photographs, journals, cards, or letters to accompany the stories? Ddo those items help you create a fuller story of the event?

Writing Prompts - United States

3. Were any lessons, habits, or traditions passed down through the generations about the war years? Consider things like storing extra food in the house, promoting peace, or watching over an adopted grave.

4. Have you sought additional information or photographs about the town(s) where you family lived during the war to add to the stories you heard?

5. When you sought additional information, did you uncover any family secrets or a story you didn't know before or that wasn't what it appeared to be?

Preserving the Memories

1. How does your family preserve the memories of those who fought and died or those who lived through the war?

2. How do you pass these memories and stories to future generations? Have you written letters, a journal, a book, compiled a photo album, or created a website?

3. Have you donated materials (photographs, letters, journals, official paperwork, military uniforms and medals, etc.) to a museum or archive? When and why?

Writing Prompts - Europe

Life Before the War

1. Describe life before the war. Consider education, jobs, and the roles of men, women and children in your family.
    a. What jobs did your father hold?
    b. Did your mother work outside the house?
    c. Did anyone in your extended family live with or near?
    d. Did the children in the family help with chores in the house or work outside the house to help support the family?

2. How did those roles change as war became more imminent?

3. How did your family earn a living prior to the war? How did that change during the war?

4. Were you able to travel freely between countries prior to the war? How did that change with the Occupation?

5. What was your town like prior to the war?

6. What was the political situation in your country prior to the war?
    a. How did this change during the war?
    b. How did this change after the war?

7. Did your family have a tradition of military service? If so, who served and in what wars or conflicts?

8. What kind of entertainment did the family enjoy prior to the war? Radio, movies, museums, picnics, etc.

9. Describe the clothing, hair, and shoe styles prior to the war. Do you have photographs to illustrate how your family dressed? Did your family wear the latest fashions?

10. Describe the technology available prior to the war.
    a. How did this change during the war? What new technology became available?
    b. How did this change after the war? What new technology became available?

Occupation Or Annexation?

1. What was your town like prior to the Occupation?

2. Was your town occupied or annexed by the Germans? Describe how this changed life in your town.

3. How were the citizens of the town treated during the war?

4. If the way your family made a living changed during the occupation, explain the change.

5. What kind of rationing took place during the war? Did this change after Liberation?

6. What kind of travel restrictions did your family face during the occupation?

7. What events or battles took places in your town during the war?

8. What was your town like during the invasion of Allied troops? Who liberated your town?

9. How were the citizens treated during the invasion of Allied troops? Were they asked to leave the town or were they able to remain?

10. If your family's city was bombed, how did they handle that?

11. If your family was forced to evacuate during a battle, where did they go? How did they survive? At what point were they allowed to return to their homes? And, was anything left?

12. How did your town change after the war ended?

Writing Prompts - Europe

Propaganda

1. Describe the propaganda from the war and how that impacted your family.

2. Where did you find propaganda? In the newspapers, magazines, radio, posters, rallies, training for military or civilian service?
   a. Were you allowed to have a radio during the war?

3. How did that help or hinder support for the war or anger toward the enemy?

4. Did anyone in your family help create propaganda during the war? Speak at a war bond drive or on the radio? Write an article for the newspaper or a magazine

Civilian Stories

1. What was life like for your family during the war? What stories were passed down?

2. How did your family cope with food shortages, bombings, fear, lack of necessary supplies, loss of property, loss of family?

3. What after effects of the war were passed down? Food storage, fear of attack, etc.

4. What roles did each member of your family play during the war? Soldier, nurse, wife, child, resistance member, prisoner, etc.

5. How did the roles of women change during the war?

6. How did those role changes affect the family? Which roles were forced, meaning a civilian had to go work for the Germans or fight against their will?

7. Did anyone from your town participate in the resistance movement? Who and how did they aid the war effort?

Writing Prompts - Europe

8. Was anyone from your town send to a forced labor or concentration camp? Who and under what circumstances did this happen?

9. What happened to the family property, home, village or city during the war?

10. What happened after the war? Did people talk about it? Did they share it with their children and grandchildren?

11. If soldiers returned home during the fighting, how did they cope with the trauma of war and changes at home?

12. How did the families cope with the war and all the changes and destruction it brought?

13. What kind of jobs were available before the war? During? After?

Military Service

1. If your relative served in the military, for which country, branch of service, and theater of war?

2. Discuss basic training and other specialized training through which your soldier went after being inducted in the service.

3. Write about the gear your soldier typically carried.

4. Do you have any letters, diaries, photographs, or post cards from your military soldier? Write about their service using these items.

5. Describe the living conditions of your soldier during their military service. Did he or she sleep in a tent; barracks; bombed out buildings; on the frozen ground? How often did they get a hot meal or a shower?

6. If your relatives taken as a Prisoner of War, describe their experience. If they survived the war, what was their life like post-war?

Writing Prompts - Europe

7. Describe the down time during the war, when the front line had moved or there was no battle to fight. What did your soldier do to pass the time?

8. Describe any illnesses, accidents, or wounds your soldier received during the war.

9. If your soldier died in service, describe his death based on the information you have.
    a. Were any personal effects returned to the family? Which ones? Do you still have them?
    b. What is the story behind them?

Resistance

1. What was the role of your family member or community member in the resistance?

2. How did their work help the war effort?

3. If the resistance member survived the war, did they ever talk about their work?

4. In what countries did they conduct operations or missions?

5. How did the resistance help wounded, lost, or dead Allied soldiers?

6. If the resistance member died during the war, were the remains recovered? Did the family know what happened to the resistance member?

7. How did the rest of the family handle one or more family members being involved in the resistance? Was the family ever questioned?

8. Was your resistance family member honored or memorialized after the war? Is there an annual ceremony to remember their contribution to the war?

Writing Prompts - Europe

What Would You Do?

Historical context is important when we examine events of the past. This means we examine the events through the eyes of someone living in that time and place. We do not judge based on how we live today and the choices and opportunities we have now.

Scenario 1: There were many times during the war when the Germans entered a locale to take over. Where factories or necessary buildings existed, they might have given the owner the option to work for the Germans or close the factory and send the workers to Germany to work.

This begs the question – Whose side were they on if they chose to work for the Germans? And, what would you have done?

Did this happen in your community? What was the response? How did this change your community during and after the war?

Scenario 2: Many communities had Jews living in them. How did your family view Jews prior to and during the war? Were they friends with Jewish families? What happened to those families? Did your family remain quiet about hidden Jews or did they turn people in out of fear?

Scenario 3: There is a concept of collective guilt, primarily in reference to the Germans or Japanese, in which the entire population should be held responsible for the atrocities committed during the war and for the war itself. Do you agree or disagree?

Also consider the "Sins of the father," in which the children of the "enemy" carry the shame, guilt, grief, and atrocities committed by their parents. Was this something that happened in your family?

Writing Prompts - Europe

Persecution

1. Describe any persecution in your town prior to the war.

2. If members of your family were persecuted in any way during the war, explain how and what happened. Were they sent to a camp? Executed? Disappeared without a trace?

3. How did your family cope with this?

4. How do you remember those who died, today?

Holocaust

1. Did you or your family live in a town in which many individuals were forced to leave?
    a. What was the town's name?
    b. How did that change the town?
    c. How did that change your family?

2. Did your family experience antisemitism prior to the war and if so, how?

3. How did the rise of antisemitism affect your family when the war began?

4. How did antisemitism affect your family when the war was over?

5. Did your family try to emigrate to another country in Europe or the U.S. during the 1930s?
    a. Did they succeed? If so, where did they go and when?

6. Was your family moved from their home into a ghetto? What was their experience in the ghetto?

7. Were any members of your family sent to labor or concentration camps? When and why?
    a. Were they in more than one camp? Which ones and when?
    b. Were they separated or allowed to remain together?

Writing Prompts - Europe

8. Did any survive and if so, who? What happened to them after the war?

9. What kind of work did your family members have to do in the camp?

10. How did they handle the hunger, cold, lack of clothing, illness, and death?

11. Did the members who left ever return?

12. For those that did not, do you know what happened to them? Were you able to recover their remains?

13. Who liberated the camp where your family was held? When was the camp liberated?

14. For those that returned, how was their life changed?
    a. How did they start their lives over? Where did they live and how did they survive?
    b. Emotionally? Mentally? Physically?
    c. How did they deal with these changes?
    d. How did that change the life of your family?

15. Did those who returned remain in touch with people they met in the camp?
    a. Who were those individuals?
    b. How long did they remain in touch?

16. Are those who never returned remembered in the towns from which they vanished? How and when?

Major Battles

1. What major battles took place in your town or the area in which you lived?

2. How did those battles affect the life of your family?

Writing Prompts - Europe

3. Did your family have to relocate during the battle? If so, where did they go and when were they allowed to return?

4. If your family remained in the town during the battle, what took place?

5. If your family was involved in recovery of war dead after the battle, how did that affect them? What was their experience?

6. Who liberated your town? When was it liberated? Do you celebrate the liberation today?

7. How long did it take to rebuild your town after the war?

After The War

1. What happened after the war? Did people talk about it? Did they share it with their children and grandchildren?

2. Did the soldiers who returned home keep their weapons, uniforms, medals, war souvenirs? Did these items get passed down through the generations? Were the stories surrounding these items shared?

3. Was the area in which your family lived rebuilt? How long did it take to rebuild?

4. If your family was involved in recovery of war dead after the battle, how did that affect them? What was their experience?

5. What kind of jobs were available before the war? During? After?

6. How did the roles of women change during the war?

7. How or did your family resume a normal life?

Writing Prompts - Europe

8. Describe movement during the war and after the war.
    a. Did any of your family members move from the city to the country or vice versa?
    b. Did any of your family members immigrate to another country after the war?

9. How did the soldiers cope with the trauma of war?
10. How did the families cope with the trauma of war?

11. What about those who died – were they recovered? Where are they buried?

12. Did any of your family's soldiers remain in service? Who? What branch? How long did they serve?

13. What lessons did the family pass down about the war, the aftermath, and their lives?

War Orphans and Adoption

1. If your father killed in the war as a soldier, civilian, member of the resistance, or other way, did your mother remarry? How did you feel about that?

2. If your mother remarried after the war and your step-father adopted, how did you feel about that?

3. If your mother did not remarry, how did she support you and, if applicable, your siblings? Did she move back in with her family?

4. Was your deceased father discussed as you grew up or was it a topic that was not discussed? Explain.

5. When did you learn about your father's service? What information, stories, or photographs helped you piece together his story?

Memories of Post-War Generations

1. What memories do you have of your parents, grandparents, or other family members telling you about the war? What stories did they tell you?

2. Do you have any photographs, journals, cards, or letters to accompany the stories? Do those items help you create a fuller story of the event?

3. What lessons, habits, or traditions passed down through the generations about the war years? Consider things like storing extra food in the house, promoting peace, or watching over an adopted grave.

4. Have you sought additional information or photographs about the town(s) where you family lived during the war to add to the stories you heard? What did you uncover?

5. When you sought additional information, did you uncover any family secrets or a story you didn't know before or that wasn't what it appeared to be? Describe what you learned and the effect it had on the family when the knowledge was revealed.

Preserving the Memories

1. How does your family preserve the memories of those who fought and died or those who lived through the war?

2. How do you preserve the memories of those who were persecuted and never returned home?

3. How do you pass these memories and stories to future generations? Have you written letters, a journal, a book, compiled a photo album, or created a website?

4. Does your family carry on traditions that were done prior to and during the war? Which ones and why? If not, why not?

5. Have you donated materials (photographs, letters, journals, official paperwork, military uniforms and medals, etc.) to a museum or archive? When and why?

Grave Adoption and American Military Research

1. Did your parents or other relatives adopt graves? What are the stories and reasons for grave adoption in your family?

2. Were any of the adopted graves passed down through the family?

3. Have you adopted a grave? If so, did you choose the grave you adopted for a specific reason?

4. How often do you visit the graves?

5. Do you also volunteer at the cemeteries?

6. Are you involved in any organizations for grave adoption?

7. Do you research the service and families of your adopted soldiers?
    a. What have your research goals been for each soldier?
    b. What resources did you use to locate information? Family, Ancestry.com, Fold3.com, websites, libraries, museums, U.S. National Archives, European archives, U.S. researchers?
    c. Are you involved in any organizations for military research?

8. Did you meet your research goals? How long did it take?

9. Have you traveled to the U.S. to meet veterans, families, or do research? When and what did you do?

10. Have you written and shared the soldier's story? How?

11. Do you teach your children or grandchildren (if applicable) about your soldier? How?

Writing Prompts - Europe

12. Are you in touch with the soldier's families?

13. Have you met the soldier's family in person in Europe or America?

14. Are there photos and letters saved from correspondence between the European family and American family?

15. Do you have any of the soldier's possession? How did you get them? From whom? What are they, what is their significance and are there stories attached to those items?

Walking the Battlefields Today

1. Are you or members of your family involved in metal detecting? What artifacts have you found? What do you do with them when you find them?

2. If you find artifacts on the battlefields that have some identifiable information you can use to track a soldier, do you? Do you try to return the item to the soldier's family? Do you try to research the soldier and learn his story?

3. Are you involved in the tracing and recovery of soldiers still Missing In Action? In what ways do you help government agencies recover remains?

4. Do you research battlefields to learn what happened there? Do you provide tours or history to visitors? Do you have a website where you disseminate information?

5. Do you participate in re-enactment groups?
    a. Which one(s)?
    b. What is your role(s) and how do you help preserve the history of the war?

Writing Prompts - Europe

Memorials and Monuments

1. Does your town have memorials or monuments for the war dead? Resistance members? To mark an Allied invasion or liberation?

2. What do the memorials and monuments look like? What details, names, dates, etc., are preserved on each?

3. Are there ceremonies each year to remember the war at the memorial or monument?

4. Are new memorials or monuments being erected today? By whom and why?

Liberation Ceremonies

1. What liberation ceremonies are held in your locale? When are they held? What occurs at the ceremonies?

2. Does the country commemorate the war dead? How? When?

3. Do you ever participate in the memorial or commemorative events? How?

4. Do U.S. and Allied veterans attend these events? What is their role?

5. What meaning do these ceremonies have for you?

6. What meaning did your soldiers give to these ceremonies, if they were held during their lifetimes?

7. Do you attend the dedication of any memorials or monuments? Why or why not?

8. Do you attend Memorial Day events at American Battle Monuments Commission Cemeteries?

Writing Prompts - Veterans

Biographical Questions

1. What is your full name?

2. Where and when were you born?

3. Who were your parents?

4. Did you have siblings? Who were they? Did any serve in the war?

5. What kind of education and experience did you have prior to entering the military?
    a. Did this affect the branch in which you enlisted or were drafted?
    b. Did this affect the MOS (job) you were given after basic training?

6. Where were you when Pearl Harbor was attacked?

7. What did you know about the war before you were inducted? Was it a part of your everyday life?

8. How did you feel about the Germans, Italians, and Japanese prior to serving in the military?
    a. Did you consider the men you fought against were similar to you with hopes, wishes, dreams, and families at home?
    b. How did this feeling change when you went to war?
    c. Were you ever able to forgive the enemy?
    d. Did you ever meet anyone you fought against?

Military Service

1. In which branch of the service did you serve? Did you choose to serve in this branch?

2. When and where were you inducted in the service?
    a. How old were you when you were inducted into service?

Writing Prompts - Veterans

3. Where were you living when you were inducted?

4. Were you single or married when you entered service? Did you get married while you were in the service?

5. Did you serve in the military prior to WWII? If so, when, where, and what branch?

6. What was your serial or service number?

7. What was your final grade or rank?

8. What was your MOS (Military Occupational Specialty)? Did it change during your service? When and why?

9. What were your first impressions of the military after induction and reporting for training?
    a. Where did you complete basic training?
    b. How were you transported to the base, fort, or station for basic training?
    c. Did you train in more than one location? What did you learn?
    d. Did you attend any service schools or ASTP?

10. How did you adapt to military life? Was it challenging?

11. Did you ever go AWOL? Under what circumstances? What happened when you returned or were caught?

12. In Which unit(s) did you serve?

13. Did you serve in the continental U.S. or did you also serve overseas?
    a. What were the dates and locations of stations overseas?
    b. Did you have a furlough to get your affairs in order at home before you shipped overseas?
    c. On furlough, what did you do? Who did you see?

14. In which theater(s) of war did you serve?

Writing Prompts - Veterans

15. In what countries did you fight overseas?
    a. What were your impressions of civilians in those countries?

16. In what campaigns did you participate?
    a. What do you remember most about those campaigns?

17. In which battles did you participate?
    a. What do you remember most about those battles?
    b. What was the weather like?
    c. What was the terrain like?
    d. What was the enemy like?

18. While you were overseas, what friends did you make?
    a. Did you marry someone from another country?
    b. Did you have children with someone from another country?

19. Did you ever encounter the resistance? Who and under what circumstances?

20. Did you become friends with any civilians? Who and under what circumstances?
    a. Where?
    b. How did they help you?
    c. How did you help them?
    d. Did you remain in touch after the war?

21. Did you receive any furlough time overseas? If so, where did you go? How long did you get?

22. What challenges did you have to overcome during service?
    a. From those challenges, what advice would you pass to others?

23. How did you spend your downtime during the war where you were not fighting a battle?

24. Did you have a child born while you were overseas?
    a. When was the first time you saw your child?
    b. How old were they when you returned home?

Writing Prompts - Veterans

25. Did you miss any major holidays or celebrations while you were in the service?
    a. Which ones?
    b. Why were they important to you?

26. Were you wounded?

27. While you were at war, what wishes, hopes, and dreams did you make for when you returned home?

28. Were you ever declared Missing In Action (MIA)? If so, what were the circumstances surrounding this status change?

29. Were you a Prisoner of War (POW)? If so, what were the circumstances surrounding becoming a prisoner?
    a. Where were you taken?
    b. Were you in more than one camp?
    c. How were you treated?
    d. Were you ill or wounded in the camp?
    e. Did you keep any records of the men in the camp with you?
    f. Did you write letters to family while you were in the camp?
    g. When were you released?
    h. Who liberated your camp?

30. Were any of your buddies wounded and didn't return to your unit?
    a. Who, when, and under what circumstances?
    b. Did you try to find them after the war?

31. Were any of your buddies Killed In Action?
    a. Who, when, and under what circumstances?
    b. Were they buried overseas or repatriated?
    c. Have you ever visited their graves?
    d. Have you ever visited their families?

32. If you were in the Navy or served aboard any ships, which ones? When were you aboard those ships? Where did you go?

33. Did you take photographs during the war? Do you still have them?

Writing Prompts - Veterans

34. Did you send letters home? Do you still have them?

35. Did you earn any medals, awards, or citations? Which ones and for what?

36. Where were you when President Roosevelt died on 12 April 1945?

37. Where were you when the war ended? What are your memories of VE Day and VJ Day?

38. When and where were you separated from service?

After the War

1. Did you have any issues adjusting back to civilian life when you returned home?
    a. Mental, physical, emotional?
    b. Did your family have any trouble adjusting to your return?
    c. If you were married, did the marriage survive after the war? Why or why not?
    d. Do you have any issues today because of what you experienced during the war?

2. Where were you living, or planning to live, after separation?

3. What were your plans after the war ended? Marriage? Job? Education?

4. Did you join any reunion groups after the war?
    a. Which group? When and where?
    b. Are you still active today?
    c. Do you think these groups are still important today?
5. Have you shared your war stories with your family? Why or why not?

6. Have you written your stories down to share with others?

7. Have you spoken to audiences about your experiences?

Writing Prompts - Veterans

8. Is there anything you remember fondly about the war? Specific people, places, or things?

9. There is the concept of collective guilt, in which the entire German population during the war should be held responsible for the atrocities committed and the war. Do you agree or disagree with this concept? Please explain.

10. What do you want people to remember about the war?

11. Have you ever returned to the places you fought or were wounded?

12. Do you have friends overseas that honor the unit in which you fought?

Writing Prompts - Children and Grandchildren of War

Children

1. What lessons (positive and negative) were passed down through the family because of the war?

2. What habits remained in the family after the war? Which habits were started because of the war or even earlier, during the Great Depression? Consider food storage, recycling, using everything until it had no use for anything.

3. What kind of fear did you experience during the war?

4. If you were born prior to the war, how was life different when the soldier was at war?

5. How did family life change when the soldier returned after the war? Did your parents remain married?

6. Did your father or mother suffer from any mental trauma because of their service? If so, how did they cope? How did you cope? How did this affect your life and the life of your family when you were grown?

7. Was there any neglect or abuse because of the trauma of war? Emotional, mental, spiritual, physical? This question applies not only to children but spouses of those who served.

8. Were there any prejudices or hatred held onto against the enemy after the war?
    a. Were these ingrained in you as a child?
    b. Did you hold onto those and pass them down to your children? Or did the cycle stop?

9. After the war, did your parents live more for "now" or the present moment rather than think too far into the future?

Writing Prompts - Children and Grandchildren

10. If your father survived the war, how did your perception of him change after you began investigating his military service? How did the military records compare to the stories you heard growing up?

11. If your father was Killed In Action,
    a. How did your mother cope? Did she remarry? Did she move in with family? How did this affect your upbringing and your future?
    b. What stories did you hear from your mother or family members about your father and his service?

12. What remnants of war were held onto that affected the way your parents raised you?

13. After World War II, men at age 18 were required to enlist or be drafted and serve a compulsory two year term of service. This lasted until the late 1950s. Then by Vietnam it was enlist or be drafted. How did the sons and grandsons of World War II veterans feel about this? How many in your family enlisted in the branch of their choice? How many were drafted?

14. What anger or resentment did your or do you still, carry around toward your father/soldier? How have you dealt with this to heal it and forgive him?

15. What anger or resentment do you carry toward your mother if she raised you without your father/soldier?

16. What do you wish your parents would have told you about the war or their military service?
    a. Why do you wish they could have talked about these things?

17. What do you wish you could ask your parents about their service or life during the war, if they were still alive?
    a. How would that help you understand your life?

Writing Prompts - Children and Grandchildren

18. Most men of the right age HAD to go fight. There was no choice. How did this lack of choice affect how they lived the rest of their lives and raised their children, if they survived the war? Did they feel they still had choices after the war?

19. How did your mother and the family cope if the father was in any way disabled (mentally, physically, emotionally) from the war?
    a. How did the family cope if he spent most of his days living in a hospital rather than with the family?
    b. How did this impact the lives of his children?

20. How did the family feel about education after the war? With the GI Bill, many men and women had the opportunity for higher education. For those who took advantage of this, how did that change the way they saw education for their children?

21. What opportunities existed for your family post-war that were not there pre-war?

22. If you had pre-war born siblings and you were a war or post-war born child, how did your relationship with your parents differ from your siblings? Think about time, affection, resources, emotions, and family dynamics.

23. If your father died in the war or was in a hospital and you were raised by your mother, how did that impact how you related to women?
    a. Did that impact the type of woman you married?
    b. How did the lack of a father figure impact your ability to be a good father and male role model?

24. If your father did not fight in the war for any reason (age, disability, job essential to the war effort, other) how did the affect him and your family? Many men were called cowards if they did not fight. Did your family encounter this?

Writing Prompts - Children and Grandchildren

25. Due to the Great Depression and the war, are there issues that spread through the generations surrounding wants, needs, lack (of money, resources, choices) and how did that affect the family?

26. If you examine your family through historical context and the military research, put yourself in their shoes. Try to understand why things were the way they were and how that affected how they dealt with life and raised their family. For the things you carry around that need to be forgiven, find answers or understanding of, closure or healing, how can you find this?

27. As you write the stories, do you see any similarities between your life and that of your parents?

Grandchildren

1. What lessons were passed down through the family because of the war?

2. What habits remained in the family after the war? Which habits were started because of the war or even earlier, during the Great Depression? Consider food storage, recycling, using everything until it had no use for anything.

3. What stories did you hear about your grandfather or grandmother who served in the war?
    a. What was your perception of that individual?
    b. How did your perception change after you started researching his or her service?

4. What remnants of war were held onto that affected the way your parents raised you?

5. Were there any prejudices or hatred held onto against the enemy after the war that your parents carried through their generation?
    a. Were these ingrained in you as a child?
    b. Did you hold onto those and pass them down to your children? Or did the cycle stop?

Writing Prompts - Children and Grandchildren

6. Was there abuse or neglect in your family because of how your parents were raised after the war? How did you cope with it? Did you allow the abuse to continue or did you stop the cycle?

7. What anger or resentment did your or do you still, carry around toward your grandfather/soldier? How have you dealt with this to heal it and forgive him? (I never realized I was angry with my grandfather for enlisting when he had a wife and three boys at home, until I compared my life as a single mom to that of my grandmother's after the war.)

8. What do you wish you could ask your grandparents about their service or life during the war, if they were still alive?
    a. How would that help you understand your life?

9. If you examine your family through historical context and the military research, put yourself in their shoes. Try to understand why things were the way they were and how that affected how they dealt with life and raised their family. For the things you carry around that need to be forgiven, find answers or understanding of, closure or healing, how can you find this?

10. As you write the stories, do you see any similarities between your life and that of your grandparents?

11. How do you feel about war? Did you serve in the military? Why or why not?

Writing Prompts – Visiting The Theaters of War

Families visiting the Theaters of War

These prompts were written with the thought of U.S. families visiting Europe based on WWII reasons.

1. What was the reason for your visit?

2. Did you travel on your own or with a group? Why did you make the choice you did?

3. Did you meet any re-enactment groups? Which ones? Explain.

4. What did you plan to see?

5. Did you attend any memorial, commemorative, or Liberation ceremonies?

6. How did it feel to attend those ceremonies?

7. Who did you plan to meet and why?

8. Who else did you meet you were not expecting?

9. Did you see everything you planned to see? Explain.

10. Did you see things or have unexpected experiences? Explain.

11. What were the best parts of the trip?

12. What did you learn about your soldier's story or service?

13. Did you walk where your soldier fought and, if applicable, died?

14. How did it feel to walk where your soldier walked?

15. Did you visit any museums created specifically for your soldier's unit or battles in which he fought?

16. Were you able to find answers to questions you had about your soldier's service?

17. Did you find any forgiveness, healing and closure on the trip?

18. Will you go back? Why or why not?

Veterans Visiting the Theaters of War

1. What was the reason for your visit?

2. Did your family go with you?

3. Did you travel on your own or with a group? Why did you make the choice you did?

4. Did you meet any re-enactment groups?

5. What did you plan to see?

6. Did you attend any memorial, commemorative, or Liberation ceremonies?

7. How did it feel to attend those ceremonies?

8. Who did you plan to meet and why?

9. Who else did you meet you were not expecting?

10. Did you see everything you planned to see?

11. Did you see things or have unexpected experiences?

Writing Prompts - Visiting Theaters of War

12. How did it feel to be where you fought? Were you wounded? Did you visit that site?

13. Did you visit any American Battle Monument Commission Cemeteries and your fallen buddies? Describe the visit, emotions, and who you visited. What was your buddy's story?

14. Were you treated like a returning hero by those you met? How did that feel?

15. What were the best parts of the trip?

16. Did you visit any museums created specifically for your unit or battles in which you fought?

17. Did you learn about your service you had forgotten or did not know?

18. Did you find any forgiveness, healing and closure on the trip?

Additional Resources

Additional Resources

The book list provided here are books I have on my shelf that have inspired me to write silly and serious stories. A few are related to oral history, citing sources, or writing about war.

Ackerman, Angela and Puglisi, Becca. The Emotion Thesaurus: A Writer's Guide to Character Expression. The Bookshelf Muse: 2012.

Alderson, Martha. The Plot Whisperer Book of Writing Prompts. Avon: F+W Media, 2013.

Barnes, Nancy. Stories to Tell. Redding, CA: Stories To Tell, 2010.

Cameron, Julia. The Artist's Way. New York: Penguin, 2002.

Capps, Ron. Writing War A Guide to Telling Your Own Story. (See his website http://veteranswriting.org/)

Carmack, Sharon DeBartolo. You Can Write Your Family History. Baltimore: Genealogical Publishing Company reprint, 2008.

Donovan, Melissa. 101 Creative Writing Exercises. San Francisco: Swan Hatch Press, 2011.

Dowrick, Stephanie. Creative Journal Writing. New York: Penguin, 2009.

Franco, Carlo and Lineback, Kent. The Legacy Guide. New York: Penguin, 2006.

Ellis, Sherry, editor. Now Write! Nonfiction. New York: Penguin, 2009.

Funk, Charles Earle. Heavens to Betsy & Other Curious Sayings. New York: Harper, reprint 1983.

Goldberg, Natalie. Old Friend from Far Away. New York: Free Press, 2007.

Additional Resources

Goldberg, Natalie. Writing Down the Bones. Boston: Shambhala, 2005.

Hart, Cynthia with Samson, Lisa. The Oral History Workshop. New York: Workman Publishing, 2009.

Hatcher, Patricia Law. Producing a Quality Family History. Salt Lake City: Ancestry Inc., 1996.

Hale, Constance. Vex, Hex, Smash, Smooch. Let Verbs Power Your Writing. New York: Norton and Company, 2012.

Hart, Cynthia with Samson, Lisa. The Oral History Workshop. New York: Workman Publishing, 2009.

Hart, Jack. Story Craft The Complete Guide to Writing Narrative Nonfiction. Chicago: University of Chicago Press, 2012.

Heffron, Jack. The Writer's Idea Book . Cincinnati: Writer's Digest Books, 2011.

Kazemek, Francis. Exploring Our Lives. Santa Monica, CA: Santa Monica Press, 2002.

Kramer, Mark and Call, Wendy, editors. Telling True Stories. New York: Penguin, 2007.

LaPlante. The Making of a Story. A Norton Guide to Creative Writing. New York: W.W. Norton and Company, 2007.

LeDoux, Denis. Turning Memories into Memoirs. Lisbon Falls: Soleil Press, 2006.

Oliver, Laura. The Story Within. New York: Penguin, 2011.
Oriah Mountain Dreamer. What We Ache For. San Francisco: Harper, 2005.

Polking, Kirk. Writing Family Histories and Memoirs. Cincinnati: Betterway Books, 1995.

Additional Resources

Reeves, Judy. A Writer's Book of Days. Novato: New World Library, 2010.

Reeves, Judy. Writing Alone Writing Together A Guide for Writers and Writing Groups. Novato: New World Library, 2002.

San Francisco Writers' Grotto. 642 Things To Write About. San Francisco: Chronicle Books, 2011.

Schawrz, Ted. The Complete Guide to Writing Biographies. Cincinnati: Writer's Digest Books, 1990.

Shown Mills, Elizabeth. Evidence Explained. Baltimore: Genealogical Publishing Company, 2009.

Starfire, Amber Lea. Week by Week A Year's Worth of Journaling and Meditation Prompts. Napa, CA: MoonSkye Publishing, 2011.

Szabados, Stephen. Write Your Family History. Stephen Szabados: IL, 2014.

About The Author

Spiritual Coach, Intuitive healer specializing in inherited & war trauma, and personal & ancestral healing.

I'm a spiritual coach and an Intuitive healer specializing in inherited & war trauma, and personal & ancestral healing. I've been on a conscious personal healing journey for a more than a decade. My journey began over 25 years ago while researching & writing about my family & military history. My military ancestors helped me dive deeper into my personal & ancestral trauma to heal.

Discovering the history of our families allows for family patterns, inherited trauma, & secrets to rise. This provides an opportunity to take a deeper look at our research to allow for healing & closure.

By 2015 my healing journey & military work allowed me to travel in Europe & create a life both there & in Chicago. I became embedded in Dutch society, life, relationships, healthcare, politics, culture, got a deep dive into grief when I became a caregiver to someone I was married to in the Netherlands. All of that gave me a unique perspective on our world & the layers of trauma we each carry, no matter where we live.

I visited battlefields & burial sites, religious & cultural sites, heard family & war stories, some of which brought me to my knees in grief as I channeled the people telling the stories. I understand context that many people do not. This makes me unique in the way I can help clients heal on both sides of the ocean to explore their personal & ancestral family patterns & war trauma. I have studied & understand genealogy & military records, & what information, secrets, patterns, inherited trauma, feelings, & emotions they may share.

Each experience I had in Europe gave me awareness & puzzle pieces for my healing & the healing of our ancestors & the collective. Puzzle pieces & awareness I can now share with you.

For more than a decade I have studied ancestral lineage healing, energy healing modalities, inherited trauma, PTSD, grief & loss, caregiving, & spiritual modalities. I have also taken a deep dive into my personal and ancestral healing.

I look forward to working with you to heal yourself and your ancestors. We are all connected no matter where we live, what our culture is, what our trauma has been….when one heals, we all heal.

You can learn more at:
Ancestral Souls Wisdom School
https://www.ancestralsoulswisdomschool.com

WWII Research & Writing Center
http:/wwiirwc.com

www.ingramcontent.com/pod-product-compliance
Lightning Source LLC
Chambersburg PA
CBHW061506040426
42450CB00008B/1505